P9-CUK-131

American Holidays

COLUMBUS DAY

Connor Dayton

PowerKiDS press.
New York

Published in 2012 by The Rosen Publishing Group, Inc.
29 East 21st Street, New York, NY 10010

First Edition

Editor: Jennifer Way
Book Design: Julio Gil

Photo Credits: Cover, p. 21 Spencer Platt/Getty Images; pp. 5, 24 (top left) SuperStock/Getty Images; p. 7 Shutterstock.com; p. 9 Universal History Archive/Getty Images; pp. 11, 24 (bottom) Kean Collection/Getty Images; p. 13 Apic/Getty Images; p. 15 Photos.com/Thinkstock; p. 17 Timothy A. Clary/AFP/Getty Images; pp. 19, 23, 24 (top right) Mario Tama/Getty Images.

Library of Congress Cataloging-in-Publication Data

Dayton, Connor.
Columbus Day / by Connor Dayton. — 1st ed.
p. cm. — (American holidays)
Includes index.
ISBN 978-1-4488-6145-3 (library binding) — ISBN 978-1-4488-6248-1 (pbk.) —
ISBN 978-1-4488-6249-8 (6-pack)
1. Columbus Day—Juvenile literature. 2. Columbus, Christopher—Juvenile literature. 3. America—Discovery and exploration—Spanish—Juvenile literature. I. Title.
E120.D39 2012
394.264—dc23
2011024985

Manufactured in the United States of America

CPSIA Compliance Information: Batch #WW12PK: For Further Information contact Rosen Publishing, New York, New York at 1-800-237-9932

Contents

Columbus Day honors the **explorer** Christopher Columbus.

Columbus was from Genoa, in today's Italy.

Switzerland
Slovenia
Croatia
Bosnia - Herzegovina
Genoa
Italy
France
Montenegro
Adriatic Sea
Corsica
Tyrrhenian Sea
Sardinia
Sicily

In 1492, Columbus sailed from Spain. He wanted to get to India by crossing the Atlantic Ocean.

Columbus had three **ships**. They were the *Niña,* the *Pinta,* and the *Santa María*.

Columbus saw land on October 12, 1492. He thought he had reached Asia.

He called these islands the West Indies. He called the people Indians.

Columbus Day is the second Monday in October.

Columbus Day **parades** honor both the explorer and Italian Americans.

ITALIAN - ENGLISH
DUAL LANGUAGE
PROGRAM
BUSES
& RIGHT TURNS
ONLY
7AM-7PM
MON THRU FRI
ITALIAN - ENGLISH
DUAL LANGUAGE PROGRAM
JEFFERSON ELEMENTARY SCHOOL
NEW ROCHELLE, N.Y.

New York City has the biggest Columbus Day parade.

24

What do you do on Columbus Day?

Words to Know

explorer

parade

ships

Index

Web Sites

Due to the changing nature of Internet links, PowerKids Press has developed an online list of Web sites related to the subject of this book. This site is updated regularly. Please use this link to access the list:
www.powerkidslinks.com/amh/columbus/